READING JAZZ

The New Method for Learning to Read Written Jazz Music

by Jacques Rizzo

Alfred Music Publishing Co., Inc.
P.O. Box 10003
Van Nuys, CA 91410-0003
alfred.com

ISBN-10: 0-7692-1425-8 (Book & CD)
ISBN-13: 978-0-7692-1425-2 (Book & CD)

Design/Layout: NINA LLOPIS

Reading Jazz
CD Tracking Sheet

		Time			**Time**
1.	Duet 1 - Preliminary Exercise	:41	41. Duet 14 - Preliminary Exercise		1:19
2.	Duet 1 - First Time	:58	42. Duet 14 - Preliminary Exercise		2:17
3.	Duet 2 - Preliminary Exercise 1	:29	43. Duet 14 - Preliminary Exercise		3:18
4.	Duet 2 - Preliminary Exercise 2	:34	44. Duet 14 - Say It Again, Virginia D.		1:09
5.	Duet 2 - Preliminary Exercise 3	:23	45. Duet 15 - Preliminary Exercise		:19
6.	Duet 2 - The Smoothie	1:54	46. Duet 15 - Two Brothers		1:14
7.	Duet 3 - Preliminary Exercise 1	:25	47. Duet 16 - Preliminary Exercise		1:19
8.	Duet 3 - Preliminary Exercise 2	:37	48. Duet 16 - Preliminary Exercise		2:17
9.	Duet 3 - Daht's Dah Vay	1:10	49. Duet 16 - Two Others		1:02
10.	Duet 4 - Preliminary Exercise 1	:37	50. Duet 17 - Preliminary Exercise		1:22
11.	Duet 4 - Preliminary Exercise 2	:24	51. Duet 17 - Preliminary Exercise		2:21
12.	Duet 4 - Pop It!	1:15	52. Duet 17 - Cha - Da!		:46
13.	Duet 5 - Preliminary Exercise 1	:24	53. Duet 18 - Preliminary Exercise		:19
14.	Duet 5 - Preliminary Exercise 2	:23	54. Duet 18 - Bleu Skies		1:08
15.	Duet 5 - Slip "N Slide	1:29	55. Duet 19 - Preliminary Exercise		:20
16.	Duet 6 - Preliminary Exercise	:23	56. Duet 19 - Just For Jack		1:05
17.	Duet 6 - One More Time	2:00	57. Duet 20 - Preliminary Exercise		:36
18.	Duet 7 - Preliminary Exercise 1	:22	58. Duet 20 - Egual Octavo		1:18
19.	Duet 7 - Preliminary Exercise 2	:21	59. Duet 21 - Preliminary Exercise		:23
20.	Duet 7 - Preliminary Exercise 3	:19	60. Duet 21 - Bright Eyes		1:35
21.	Duet 7 - Same Lick - Different Look	1:29	61. Duet 22 - Preliminary Exercise		:30
22.	Duet 8 - Preliminary Exercise 1	:20	62. Duet 22 - Barbara's Blues		1:42
23.	Duet 8 - Preliminary Exercise 2	:20	63. Duet 23 - Preliminary Exercise		:25
24.	Duet 8 - Skippin'	1:10	64. Duet 23 - Jersey's Bounce		1:25
25.	Duet 9 - Preliminary Exercise 1	:19	65. Duet 24 - Preliminary Exercise		:22
26.	Duet 9 - Preliminary Exercise 2	:20	66. Duet 24 - Kickin' It Around		1:21
27.	Duet 9 - Two Short - Not Too Short	1:11	67. Duet 25 - Preliminary Exercise		1:34
28.	Duet 10 - Preliminary Exercise 1	:21	68. Duet 25 - Preliminary Exercise		2:20
29.	Duet 10 - Preliminary Exercise 2	:19	69. Duet 25 - Charlie Jack		1:24
30.	Duet 10 - Preliminary Exercise 3	:19	70. Duet 26 - Preliminary Exercise		:21
31.	Duet 10 - The Frondescence of Fall	1:16	71. Duet 26 - September's Song		1:13
32.	Duet 11 - Preliminary Exercise 1	:20	72. Duet 27 - Preliminary Exercise		:21
33.	Duet 11 - Preliminary Exercise 2	:18	73. Duet 27 - Sippimissi Mud		:53
34.	Duet 11 - A Little Minor Blooze	1:23	74. Duet 28 - Preliminary Exercise		:32
35.	Duet 12 - Preliminary Exercise 1	:21	75. Duet 28 - Melody For Michelle		1:13
36.	Duet 12 - Preliminary Exercise 2	:19	76. Duet 29 - Preliminary Exercise		:24
37.	Duet 12 - A Ol' Ian	1:31	77. Duet 29 - Lull-A-Byin' Rhythm		1:21
38.	Duet 13 - Preliminary Exercise 1	:21	78. Duet 30 - Preliminary Exercise		:29
39.	Duet 13 - Preliminary Exercise 2	:17	79. Duet 30 - Triplication		1:53
40.	Duet 13 - Restin, Fore and Aft	1:05			

Total   57:37

PREFACE

How This Text Can Help You

Throughout the country, thousands of music educators spend untold hours teaching jazz ensemble music by rote as, with few exceptions, students entering their bands have only had traditional, classically oriented training. Few are able to read written jazz music accurately, no less interpret the parts using idiomatic articulations.

This was also my situation, even though the members of the jazz ensemble were the best musicians in the school at which I taught. It was difficult to find time in an already overcrowded schedule to teach reading and interpretation of written jazz music. This self-study text and tape was developed in answer to this problem. I say self-study as most of the students using it were able to work through the duets by themselves with little or no help on my part. Indeed, the play-along format made learning to play in a jazz style easy and enjoyable. Completion of this text is now a prerequisite to membership in the jazz ensemble and excerpts from the duets are used for auditions. The result is that, from the first rehearsal, students are not only reading music, but working toward making it "swing."

Although designed for scholastic use, the text may be of assistance to classical musicians who find themselves called upon to perform works in the jazz idiom, and music educators with little or no jazz experience who wish to conduct jazz ensembles or works in a jazz style.

Why Jazz Music Is Difficult to Read

Traditionally trained musicians encounter difficulty in reading jazz for three reasons. First, the rhythm patterns, although written in four quarter time with an even subdivision of the beat, are usually performed with an uneven subdivision of the beat. Secondly, performance of these rhythm patterns is complicated by an inconsistency in their notation by jazz arrangers and composers. One pattern may be written in several different ways, all of which are to be performed in an identical manner. Lastly, the phrasing and articulation are often poorly notated, if notated at all, the arranger assuming the performer will interpret the music with characteristic phrasing and articulation. It is to these three problems that this text is addressed.

How the Text Was Written

The rhythm patterns selected for use in this text were drawn from over four hundred pages of written jazz music currently in print. Any rhythm pattern that appeared three or more times was included in the book. These rhythm patterns were sorted into fourteen categories with one category (syncopated quarter notes) having thirteen subdivisions. The rhythm patterns are presented in the text in order of increasing complexity.

Prior to writing the duets, five intermediate method books were analyzed with regard to range, key signatures, note and rest values used, etc. This survey was used as a guide in limiting the technical difficulty of the duets.

There is a considerable range in the number of articulation marks supplied in the parts, from preliminary exercises in which every note is marked to duets in which there are few (if any) markings. This was done to simulate the wide variety in the amount of articulative markings to be found in the music students will play.

Final revisions were made after two years of use with students from two different school systems. The duets were rated by four prominent jazz educators representing middle school through collegiate levels in categories developed by the National Association of Jazz Educators. The consensus of these ratings was (1) grade of difficulty (rated I-VII): III/IV, or medium difficulty, and (2) musical rating (rated A-F): A minus, or excellent. It was also noted that articulations used conformed to the Standardization of Stage Bands Articulations recommended by NAJE.

INTRODUCTION

This text is designed to help you read written jazz rhythm patterns accurately using idiomatic articulations. The most commonly used jazz rhythm patterns are presented, one at a time, in order of increasing complexity in a series of duets. Each duet is preceded by an introductory section to guide you in your initial approach to the rhythm patterns. This introduction is divided into five parts: Heading, Written, Played, Preliminary Exercises, and Review.

Heading. The rhythm patterns presented in each duet is stated in the heading. Careful reading of the heading will help you understand the arrangement of the notes that form each pattern.

Written. Directly below the heading, the musical notation (and any alternate notations) of the rhythm pattern is shown, with reference to a particular measure in the duet where that rhythm pattern may be found. Compare the various alternate notations, one to another, to understand how notes of different duration are used in conjunction with rests and ties to write the same rhythm pattern in different ways. Also, compare the notation of particular measures in the duet to which you are referred. These comparisons will help you develop an understanding of the manner in which the various alternate notations are used.

Played. This section explains the articulation of the rhythm patterns with regard to (1) the duration of the notes that comprise the pattern, (2) the manner in which the notes are to be attacked and/or released, and (3) the accentuation of any particular tones within the pattern.

Preliminary Exercises. These exercises provide an initial approach to playing the patterns. A short heading is often included as an aid to your understanding the design or purpose of the exercise.

Cue notes above the staff are used in two ways: (1) to illustrate the uneven division of the beat (these are written on a one-line staff), or (2) as an aid to understanding the alternate notations of the pattern (these are written under a bracket). Phonetics representing the sound of the articulations are included below the staff so that you can "chant" each exercise, using "dah's" and "daht's."

Make a preliminary study of each exercise to make certain you understand the purpose of the exercise (check the heading) and the way in which the patterns are notated (check the cue notes above the staff). Each exercise should be practiced in three ways. First, listen to the recording while following the music. Second, "chant" the exercise, using phonetics. Tap your toe to the beat while chanting. Careful attention to the articulations with regard to emphasis and inflection will help you get the "feeling" of each figure. DO NOT SKIP THIS STEP. IT IS IMPORTANT THAT YOU REPEAT THIS STEP UNTIL YOU HAVE THE PATTERN "SKIPPING" ALONG — REALLY SWINGING. Lastly, play the pattern on your instrument. Again, repeat this step, matching your articulation to that on the recording, until you have the figures "swinging."

Review. This section is used to alert you to the second and third appearance of a rhythm pattern in the duets. Reference is made to a particular measure where the pattern may be found, and the duet in which the pattern first appeared.

Studying the Duets. Approach the duets in the same manner as the preliminary exercises. First, analyze the rhythm patterns while listening to the recording. Second, practice chanting the phonetics while tapping your toe and fingering the notes you are chanting on your instrument. Concentrate on the articulation. Again, this second step is most important. REPEAT THIS STEP UNTIL THE FINGERING MOVES EFFORTLESSLY AND THE CHANTING "SWINGS." Lastly, play the duet on your instrument, matching the articulation to that on the recording.

Practice Both Parts. Part I is on the left channel and Part II is on the right channel; the rhythm section is on both channels. After you have Part I really "swinging," turn off the left channel and play Part I by yourself with Part II and the rhythm section on the right channel. Practice Part II in a similar manner, turning off the right channel and playing with Part I and the rhythm section after the figures are "swinging."

The Table of Contents forms an index of the first three appearances of a particular rhythm pattern in the duets, and may be used as a guide to work on a particular pattern you feel needs practice.

Class Applications. The duets may be used for class instruction as the various parts — C treble clef, Bb, Eb, and bass clef — may be played together.

TABLE OF CONTENTS

6

Various rhythm patterns
from previous duets.

8

Duet 29, p. 73; m. 20.

Duet 29, p. 73; m. 31.

RELATED TOPICS

DUET 1

Quarter Notes, and Note Values
Larger than a Quarter Note

Written

♩ (Part I, measure 10),   ♩ (I, m. 3),   𝅝 (I, m. 1)

Played

Quarter notes that have no articulation marks are usually played 'short' (separated from the surrounding notes) with the tone stopped by the tongue (tongue 'daht'). Quarter notes marked tenuto (♩) are played 'long' (held for their full value) and legato tongued (tongue 'dah').

Note values larger than a quarter note are usually played long and legato tongued.

Cutoffs

The final note in a phrase is usually stopped at the beginning of its last beat to provide (1) an exact cutoff point, and (2) space for a breath. See, for example, m. 4 in the Preliminary Exercise below.

Preliminary Exercise

Important: Make sure you follow the directions found on page 4 when playing the exercises below and the duet that follows.

FIRST TIME

DUET 2

Series of Eighth Notes

Written
_____

* (I, m. 1)

Played
_____

The rhythmic basis of jazz is an uneven division of the beat in which the eighth note on the downbeat receives two-thirds of the beat and the eighth note on the upbeat on-third of the beat. That is,

is played or ; This change from the traditional even division of the beat in which each eighth note receives one-half of the beat is used in playing all eighth note patterns. **

Legato tongue each eighth note as smoothly as possible (tongue dah-da). Although unmarked eighth notes are usually legato tongued, individual eighth notes that are marked staccato (see m. 19) should be played short (tongue daht).

Balance of Parts
_____

Background parts should be played at a somewhat softer dynamic level than the melody. For example, Part II in Duet 2 should be played somewhat softer than Part I in measures 1-8 even though the same dynamic level (*mf*) is indicated in the parts. Harmony parts written in the same rhythm as the melody (see m. 9-14) should also be played at a softer dynamic level than the 'lead' part. Conversely, Part I in these instances should take the lead, playing at a louder dynamic level than the harmony part. Always listen to the other parts. Be aware of the role your part plays in relation to them and adjust your playing accordingly.

Cutoffs, continued
_____

If there are no rests at the end of a phrase, the final note, as was stated in Duet 1, is usually stopped at the beginning of its last beat. For example, the cutoff in m. 21 of Duet 2 is made at the start of the fourth beat of the measure.

_____

*The slash mark is used to show that a note, rather than a rest, falls on the beat following the two eighth notes.

**Even eighth notes are treated in later duets.

If the last note of the phrase, however, is followed by a rest, hold the note full value and cutoff at the start of the rest. The cutoff, for example, of the whole note in m. 10 is at the beginning of the first beat of m. 11.

If the first case (m. 21), the 'early' cutoff not only provides an exact cutoff point, but also important, leaves space for a breath. In the second instance (m. 10), the rest provides a breathing space so that the note may be held full value. Holding this note through to the rest maintains tension or 'life' in the musical line. Just as important, cutting the tone off exactly on the rest places emphasis on the cutoff (the first beat of m. 11), 'setting up' (or providing a dynamic preparation for) the rhythmic figure that starts on the following beat.

Preliminary Exercises

1. Uneven division of the beat.

2. Eighth notes on successive beats.

3. Staccato eighth notes; notes tied into eighth notes.

THE SMOOTHIE

DUET 3

Series of Dotted Eighth/Sixteenth Notes

Written

♪. ♪ (I, m. 2)

Played

Play the dotted eighth/sixteenth pattern with the same uneven division of the beat used with the series of eighth notes in Duet 2. Give the dotted eighth note two-thirds of the beat and the

sixteenth note one-third of the beat. That is, ♪. = ♪♪ both being played ♪♪. Use a legato tongue articulation on both notes (tongue dah-da).

Another articulation is occasionally used in which the dotted eighth note is played staccato. This articulation is used in the recording on the D.S.

Accents

In addition to staccato and tenuto marks (m. 2), several different accents are found in jazz

music. Notes marked ♪ are accented and played long (held full value). Notes marked ♪ are accented and played short (separated). Both types of accents are found in m. 10. Another type of accent, written by combining two dynamic marks, is the sfp or sfzp, indicating a loud accent (sf or sfz) followed immediately by a sudden drop to a softer volume level (p). This last type of accent is often combined with a crescendo, as in m. 14.

Preliminary Exercises

1. Uneven division of the beat.

2. Alternate articulation with staccato dotted eighth note; accents.

DAHT'S DAH VAY

DUET 4

Eighth Note Anticipations* Followed by a Rest

<u>Written</u>

⎍♪ 𝄾 (I, m. 5)

<u>Played</u>

As before, use an uneven division of the beat, giving the downbeat eighth note two-thirds of the beat and the upbeat eighth note one-third of the beat.

Play the downbeat eighth note long and the upbeat eighth note short (tongue dah-daht). Inexperienced players tend to rush through the downbeat eighth note, arriving at the upbeat eighth note too soon. Make sure you hold the downbeat eighth note a full two-thirds of abeat.

<u>Clef Signs and Key Signatures</u>

Much of the music you encounter will be written by copyists who only include clef signatures on the first staff of each page. Duet 4 and a number of subsequent duets have been written in this manner so that you may become accustomed to reading music of this type.

<u>Preliminary Exercises</u>

Note that the eighth note anticipations in Exercise 1 'feel' differently (and receive a slightly different emphasis or inflection) than those in Exercise 2, as different beats of the measure (strong versus weak) are anticipated.

1. Anticipation of the first and third beats.

2. Anticipation of the second and fourth beats.

*Notes that are written on the beat in traditional music are often 'anticipated' (written a half beat earlier) in jazz. For example ♩ ♩ ♩ 𝄾 in traditional music might be written ♩ ⎍ ▬ in jazz, the last note 'anticipating' the third beat of the measure.

POP IT!

* COMPARE THE NOTATION OF m.17 TO THAT OF m.21

DUET 5

Tied Eighth Note Anticipations

Written

♩♪ (I, m. 5), ♪♩. (I, m. 7)

Played

Use an uneven division of the beat. In this instance, ♩♪ is played ³♩♪. As with the pattern in Duet 4, care must be taken not to rush through the downbeat eighth note, arriving at the tied upbeat eighth note too soon. Be sure to hold the downbeat eighth note a full two-thirds of a beat.

When this rhythm pattern is written on the first or third beat, the second notation (♪♩.) is sometimes found. Here, a dotted quarter note is written instead of an eighth note tied to a quarter note (♪♩. instead of ♩♪♩). Play both notations the same way.

Playing Conflicting Rhythms

At the end of m. 6, Part II anticipates the first beat of the measure: Part I, in conflict with this, plays directly on the downbeat of m. 7. The player of Part I must be careful to place his note exactly on the first beat of the measure and not be influenced by the anticipation in Part II. These roles are reversed in the following measure. Here, Part II must be careful not to be influenced by the anticipation in Part I. If you have difficulty playing conflicting rhythms, practice chanting the parts using phonetics.

The Slur as a Phrase Mark

Long slurs in jazz are regarded as phrase marks and do not affect the articulation of the notes; that is, eighth notes are still legato tongued, quarter notes are played short, etc. Measures 3-8 (which are slurred) and measures 21-26 (which are not slurred) are played the same.

Preliminary Exercises

1. Anticipation of the first and third beats.

2. Anticipation of the second and fourth beats.

SLIP 'N SLIDE

DUET 6

Eighth Note Patterns Intermixed

Written

Played

Review the 'Played' sections of Duets 2, 3, and 5. Short slurs are usually played as written, i.e., slurred.

Accents

Quarter notes marked with both a 'rooftop' accent and a staccato dot ( ) are usually accented and played very short (I, m. 13).

Preliminary Exercise

Eighth note patterns intermixed; accents.

ONE MORE TIME

✳ TWO MEASURE REPEAT SIGN. PLAY THE MUSIC OF m. 40·41 IN m. 42·43, AND AGAIN IN m. 44·45.

DUET 7

Syncopated Quarter Note -- Basic Pattern

Written

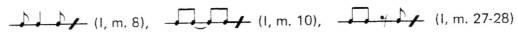 (I, m. 8), (I, m. 10), (I, m. 27-28)

There is no standardized way of notating jazz rhythm patterns--arrangers often notate the same pattern in different ways. Although the three patterns above look different, they are usually played the same.

Alternate notations of the same musical phrase are used in different places in the duets, so you may become familiar with the various ways in which the patterns are notated. Measures containing these alternate notations are cited to show how notes of different duration, rests, and ties are used to write the same pattern in different ways. Compare, for instance, Part I, m. 10 with I, m. 29, noting how the rhythm is written. Also compare II, m. 9-12 with II, m. 28-31; I, m. 20 with I, m. 24; and I, m. 32-33 with I, m. 36-37.

Played

The syncopated quarter note is played short and the eighth notes long (tongue dah-daht-dah).

Use an uneven division of the beat, the written pattern being played .

All the notations are played the same. The first notation ( ) usually occurs when the pattern starts on the first or third beat of the measure. See, for example, I, m. 8, beat three and I, m. 20, beat one.

In the second notation, ( ), the syncopated quarter note is written as two tied eighth notes (1) to allow the rhythm pattern to cross the bar line separating two measures (I, m. 13, the pattern beginning on beat 4), or (2) in order to allow the measure to be divided into two equal halves (II, m. 9, beat 2).

The third notation ( ) is similar to the pattern studied in Duet 4 -- Eighth Note Anticipations Followed by a Rest ( ). The patterns differ in that, whereas a rest of any length could follow the eighth note anticipation in Duet 4, the third notation of the syncopated quarter note pattern leaves room for only an eighth rest ( ).

Cutoffs, continued

When the last note of a phrase is tied into an eighth note which is followed by a rest( ) cutoff exactly on the eighth note; in this instance, cutoff at the start of the fourth beat. In m. 27 of the duet, the cutoff is on the eighth note at the start of the second beat.*

---

*An exception to this occurs when the chord changes on the tied eighth note. This note must then be sustained long enough for the chord to 'sound'.

Preliminary Exercises

Review the directions found on page 4 under 'Preliminary Exercises' before playing the exercises below.

1. With the pattern beginning on beats 1 or 3. Compare m. 2 with m. 3 and m. 5 with m. 6.

2. With the pattern beginning on beats 2 or 4. Compare m. 2, 3, and 4, one to another.

3. With the pattern beginning on various beats of the measure. Analyze the various alternate notations before playing.

SAME LICK-DIFFERENT LOOK

DUET 8

Syncopated Quarter Note -- with the Final Eighth Note of the
Basic Pattern Tied into a Quarter or Larger Value Note

Written

(I, m. 1),   (I, m. 25),   (I, m. 1-2)

Compare m. 1-3 with m. 32-34, and m. 5-9 with m. 24-28. In the third notation above (and
in several subsequent duets), alternate notations appear in which an eighth note tied to a quarter note is
written as a dotted quarter note.

Played

Preliminary Exercises

    1. Compare m. 1 with m. 2. Compare m. 2 with m. 4.

    2. Different notations of the same pattern beginning on various beats of the measure.
Compare m. 1-4 with m. 5-8.

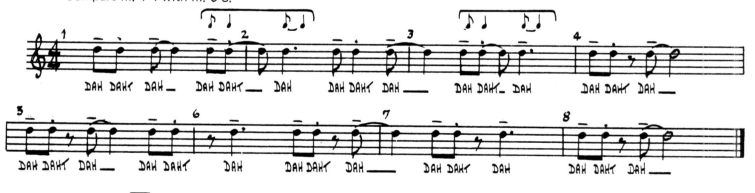

Review 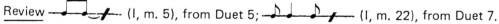 (I, m. 5), from Duet 5; (I, m. 22), from Duet 7.

SKIPPIN'

DUET 9

Syncopated Quarter Note -- with a Quarter or Larger
Value Rest Following the Basic Pattern

Written

Compare m. 13-14 to m. 17-18.   Compare m. 5, 22, and 26, one to another.   Compare m. 28, 30, and 34, one to another.

Played

Preliminary Exercises

1.   Compare m. 1 to m. 2, and m. 3 to m. 4.   Compare m. 5, 6, and 7, one to another.   Use an uneven division of the beat.

2.   Various notations of the same pattern, beginning on different beats of the measure. Compare m. 1-3 with m. 5-8.

Review

 (I, m. 6) and the alternate notation (I, m. 23) from Duet 8.

(I, m. 16), an alternate notation of from Duet 7.

TWO SHORT-NOT TOO SHORT

DUET 10

Syncopated Quarter Note -- with an Eighth Rest Substituted
for the Initial Eighth Note of the Basic Pattern

Written

Syncopated quarter notes that have no articulation marks (see above) are usually played short.

Those marked ⎯⎮⎯⎯⎯ are played long and legato tongued (II, m. 5 and 6). Those marked ⎯⎮⎯⎯ are played long and accented (I, m. 27-28).

When playing accented upbeat eighth notes (I, m. 1-2), reverse the normal tonguing pattern (tongue da-dah rather than dah-da). Use a push with the breath and diaphram rather than a tongue accent on the upbeat eighth note.

Preliminary Exercises

1. Compare m. 1 to m. 2. Use uneven beat division.

2. Both notations of the pattern beginning on various beats. Compare the articulation found in m. 1 to that found in m. 5. Also compare m. 2 with m. 6 (notation) and m. 3-4 with m. 7-8

3. Accented upbeat eighth notes.

Review

⎯⎯⎮⎯ (I, m. 15), and alternate notation of ⎯⎯⎯ from Duet 5.

THE FRONDESCENCE OF FALL

DUET 11

Syncopated Quarter Note -- Expansion of the Basic Pattern
by the Inclusion of Two Quarter Notes

Written 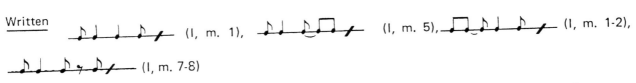 (I, m. 1), (I, m. 5), (I, m. 1-2),

(I, m. 7-8)

Compare the notation of m. 1 with m. 5, m. 7-8 with m. 11-12, and m. 17 with m. 19.

Played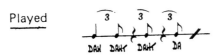
DAH DAHT DAHT DA

Preliminary Exercises

1. Compare m. 1 to m. 2, m. 2 to m. 4, and m. 5 to m. 7.

2. Different notations of the same pattern beginning on various beats of the measure. Compare m. 1 with m. 3.

Review 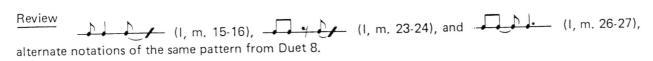 (I, m. 15-16), (I, m. 23-24), and (I, m. 26-27),
alternate notations of the same pattern from Duet 8.

A LITTLE MINOR BLOOZE

DUET 12

Syncopated Quarter Note -- with a Quarter or Larger Value Note
Tied into the Initial Eighth Note of the Basic Pattern

Written 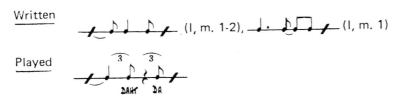 (I, m. 1-2),   (I, m. 1)

Played

Preliminary Exercises

1. Compare m. 1 to m. 2. Use an uneven beat division.

2. Both notations of the pattern played consecutively.

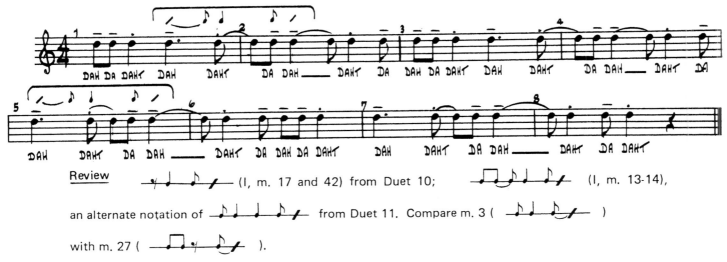

Review   (I, m. 17 and 42) from Duet 10;   (I, m. 13-14),

an alternate notation of   from Duet 11. Compare m. 3 (   )

with m. 27 (   ).

A OL' IAN

DUET 13

Syncopated Quarter Note -- with Eighth Rests Substituted
for Both Eighth Notes in the Basic Pattern

<u>Written</u>

(I, m. 5),   (I, m. 9),   (I, m. 24)

Compare the notation of m. 5, 9, and 24, one to another.

<u>Played</u>

<u>Preliminary Exercises</u>

1. Exercise with eighth rests replacing eighth notes. 'Play' these eighth rests (silently in your mind) so that you don't rush the figure, arriving at the syncopated quarter note too soon.

2. Different notations of the pattern beginning on various beats of the measure. Compare m. 1-4 with m, 5-8. 'Play' (think) the eighth rests.

RESTIN, FORE AND AFT

DUET 14

Syncopated Quarter Note -- Expansion of the Basic Pattern
by the Inclusion of Three or More Quarter Notes

Written

Pattern expanded to include three quarter notes: 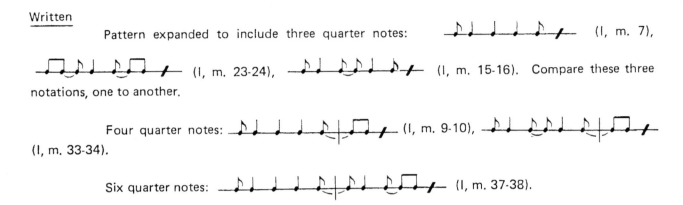 (I, m. 7), (I, m. 23-24), (I, m. 15-16). Compare these three notations, one to another.

Four quarter notes: (I, m. 9-10), (I, m. 33-34).

Six quarter notes: (I, m. 37-38).

Played

Although quarter notes in this and other patterns are usually played short, an alternate articulation is sometimes used in which the last quarter note in a series of syncopated quarter notes is played long. This articulation is used in m. 31, 33-34, and 37-38.

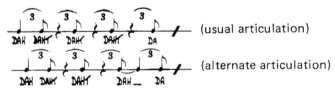

Preliminary Exercises

1. Usual articulation, uneven division of the beat.

2. Different notations of the same pattern beginning on various beats of the measure.

3. Alternate articulation with the last quarter note of the series played long.

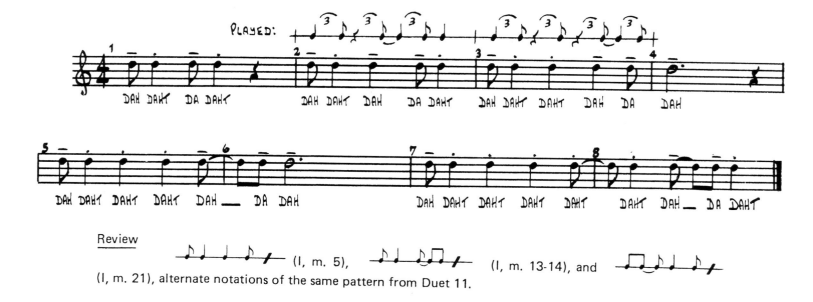

Review ♩♪♩♩♪ (I, m. 5), ♪♩♫♩ (I, m. 13-14), and ♫♩♪♩ (I, m. 21), alternate notations of the same pattern from Duet 11.

SAY IT AGAIN, VIRGINIA D.

DUET 15

Syncopated Quarter Note -- Expansion of the Pattern with an
Eighth Rest Substituted for the Initial Eighth Note
by the Inclusion of Two Quarter Notes

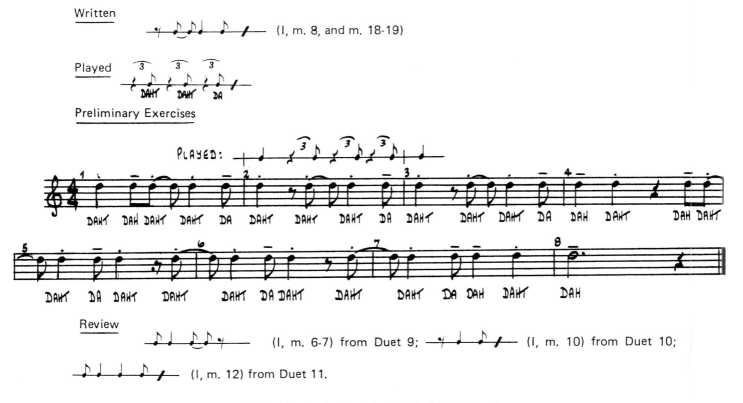

Written _____ (I, m. 8, and m. 18-19)

Played _____

Preliminary Exercises

Review _____ (I, m. 6-7) from Duet 9; _____ (I, m. 10) from Duet 10;

_____ (I, m. 12) from Duet 11.

TWO BROTHERS

DUET 16

Syncopated Quarter Note -- Expansion of the Basic Pattern
Followed by a Quarter or Larger Rest by the
Inclusion of Two or More Quarter Notes

Written

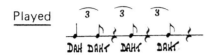

(I, m. 3), (I, m. 5-6) (I, m. 15-16).

Played

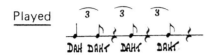

DAH DAHT DAHT DAHT

Preliminary Exercises

1. Compare m. 1 to m. 2, m. 3 to m. 4, and m. 2 to m. 4.

2. Both notations of the pattern.

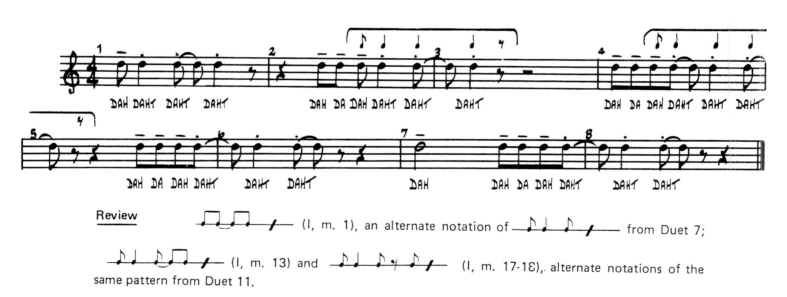

Review

(I, m. 1), an alternate notation of from Duet 7;

(I, m. 13) and (I, m. 17-18), alternate notations of the same pattern from Duet 11.

TWO OTHERS

DUET 17

Syncopated Quarter Note -- Expansion of the Pattern with
Eighth Rests Substituted for Both Eighth Notes
by the Inclusion of Three Quarter Notes

Written

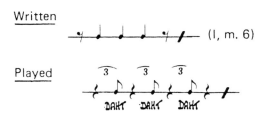 (I, m. 6)

Played

Even Eighth Notes

A series of eighth notes that lead into a climax, or the beginning of a melody or phrase, that
are marked with accents (or) or with tenuto marks ( )
are played 'evenly', i.e., with each eighth note receiving one-half of the beat. In this instance, the notes
are marked 'even' eighths (I, m. 4, 8, and 23). As they are accented, they would be (as with accented
quarter notes) played short.

Preliminary Exercises

1. With eighth rests replacing the eighth notes.

2. Even and uneven eighth note patterns. Each of the even eighth notes receives one-half
of the beat.

Review

and , alternate notations of the same pattern from

Duet 13 (I, m. 13-14, m. 15); (I, m. 13) from Duet 9.

CHA-DA!

DUET 18

Syncopated Quarter Note -- Expansion of the Pattern
with a Quarter or Larger Value Note Tied
into the Initial Eighth Note by the
Inclusion of Two Quarter Notes

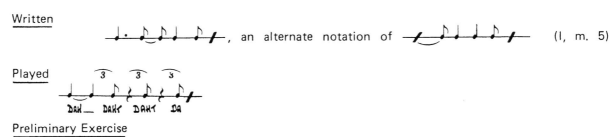

Written ⟶ , an alternate notation of ⟶ (I, m. 5)

Played

Preliminary Exercise

1. Compare m. 1 with m. 2, and m. 2 with m. 3.

Review ⟶ and ⟶ , alternate notations of the same pattern from

Duet 12 (I, m. 14-15); and , alternate notations of the

same pattern from Duet 14 (I, m. 16 and 20); from Duet 15 (I, m. 8). Compare
the rhythm pattern in m. 5 with that in m. 8.

BLEU SKIES

MODERATE SWING

DUET 19

Syncopated Quarter Note -- With a Quarter or Larger Value Note
Tied into the Initial Eighth Note of the Basic Pattern
and the Final Eighth Note Tied into
a Quarter or Larger Value Note

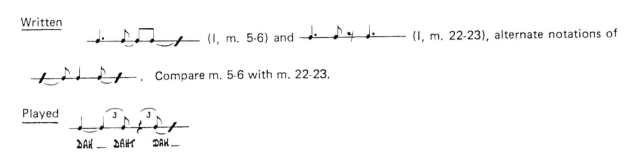

Preliminary Exercises

Compare m. 1 with m. 2; also compare m. 4-5 with m. 5-6.

Review

JUST FOR JACK

DUET 20

Even Eighth Notes in Latin American Music

Written

A variety of rhythm patterns from previous duets are used to illustrate the even eighth note articulations found in Latin American music.

Played

An even division of the beat is used, as opposed to the uneven beat division used in jazz. Series of eighth notes are played with each note receiving one-half of a beat (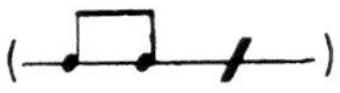), rather than the uneven beat division recommended in previous duets (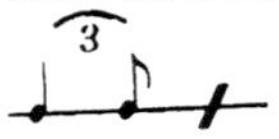). Syncopated quarter note patterns are also played evenly. For instance,  is played  (even beat division), not 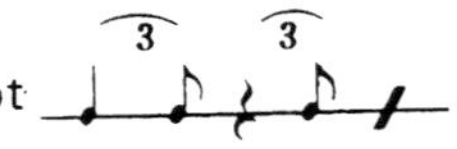 (uneven beat division).

Note values larger than a quarter note are held full value. Eighth notes may be played staccato or legato tongued and held full value. In Duet 20, staccato () or tenuto (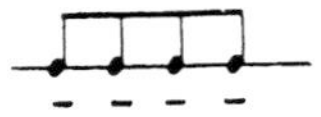) marks are used to indicate the desired articulation.

Patterns in which eighth notes and quarter notes are intermixed may be played with eighth notes long and quarter notes short as in previous duets, or an inverse articulation in which the eighth notes are played short and the quarter notes long. Thus, 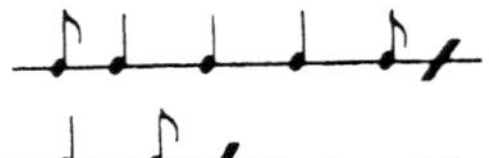 may be played  or, using an inverse articulation, 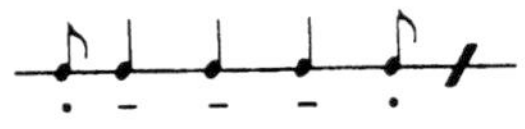 In either case, even beat division is observed. The desired articulations are marked in Duet 20.

Preliminary Exercise

Both tenuto and staccato eighth notes are used in m. 1-4; regular and inverse articulations are used in m. 5-8. Compare m. 5 with m. 7. Use an even division of the beat with all patterns.

EGUAL OCTAVO

DUET 21

Even Eighth Notes in Jazz-Rock Music

Written

A variety of rhythm patterns from previous duets are used to illustrate the even eighth note articulations found in Jazz-Rock music.

Played

As in the previous duet on Latin American music, two styles of articulation are used in playing Jazz-Rock music. In the first style, which is more often found, eighth notes are played short and quarter notes long ( ). In the second, the opposite articulation is used in which (as in jazz) the eighth notes are played long and the quarter notes short ( ). Even subdivision of the beat is used in both styles, and accent marks, slurs, etc. retain the same meaning as in previous duets.

In the duet below, m. 7-22 are played with short eighth notes and long quarters the first time, and with long eighth notes and short quarters on the repeat.

Preliminary Exercise

Compare the articulation of the first line to that of the second line.

BRIGHT EYES

1. DAH   DAH DAHT DAH___ DAHT DAHT   DAH___ DAHT DAH___ DAH   DAH___
2. DAHT   DAH DAH DAH___ DAH DAH   DAH___ DAH DAHT DAHT   DAH___

(REPEAT AD LIB. AND FADE)

DUET 22

Eighth Note Triplets

Written   (I, m. 2)

Played

    Eighth note triplets are given the same duration as in traditional music; i.e., each note of the triplet receives one-third of a beat. Each eighth note in the triplet is usually legato tongued. An alternate articulation, used especially in faster tempi, involves slurring the three notes that make up the triplet.

Preliminary Exercise

    Triplets mixed with eighth note anticipations; use an uneven division of the beat when playing the eighth note anticipations.

Review   (I, m. 26) from Duet 17;   (I, m. 24-25) from Duet 19;   (I, m. 22-23) from Duet 14.

BARBARA'S BLUES

DUET 23

Kickbeat Patterns

Written*

 (I, m. 5), (I, m. 9). Compare m. 16 with m. 18 and m. 23 with m. 25.

Played

      Accent the dotted quarter note, sustaining it for its full value. Inexperienced players, in their desire to accent the kickbeat, often rush through the eighth rest, arriving at the dotted quarter note too soon. To avoid this, concentrate on giving the rest that precedes the kickbeat note a full two-thirds of a beat. By mentally emphasizing this rest, you will achieve a strong, accurately placed accent on the kickbeat.

Preliminary Exercise

      Compare the first three measures, one to another. Mentally emphasize the rest that precedes the kickbeat note, giving it a full two-thirds of a beat.

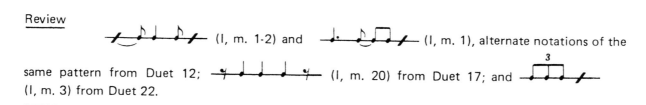

Review

 (I, m. 1-2) and (I, m. 1), alternate notations of the same pattern from Duet 12; (I, m. 20) from Duet 17; and (I, m. 3) from Duet 22.

      *The kickbeat notations shown here are similar to the notations of those syncopated quarter note patterns in which the last eighth note of the pattern is tied into a quarter note in that both notations contain a dotted quarter note on the upbeat. (See Duet 8 which contains the pattern

 notated and Duet 19 which presents the pattern notated .) The patterns differ in that, in the case of the syncopated quarter note patterns, the dotted quarter note is the second of two consecutive syncopated notes while, in the kickbeat pattern, this configuration of two consecutive syncopations is not found.

JERSEY'S BOUNCE

DUET 24

Kickbeat Patterns

Written*

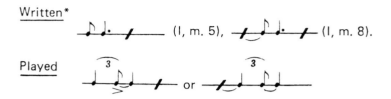 (I, m. 5), (I, m. 8).

Played

 or

Preliminary Exercise

Kickbeat note preceded by an eighth note (m. 2, 5, and 7); kickbeat note preceded by a tied eighth note (m. 3 and 6). Note that tied eighth note anticipations are found on beat 3, m. 2 and beat 1, m. 6. Use uneven beat division.

TAH   DAH DA DAH DA   DAHT TAH   DAH DAH_____   TAH   DAH DA DAH DAHT   TAH

DAH DA DAH DA DAHT TAH   DAH DAH_____ TAH   DAH DA DAH DA DAHT TAH   DAH DA DAH DAHT

Review

_____ (I, m. 23), kickbeat pattern from Duet 23; _____ (I, m. 6) not a kickbeat pattern but a syncopated quarter note pattern from Duet 19; _____ (I, m. 8), not a kickbeat pattern but a tied eighth note anticipation from Duet 5; _____ (I, m. 15) from Duet 22; _____ (I, m. 1-2) from Duet 10; _____ (I, m. 4) from Duet 17. Compare the notation of the syncopated quarter note pattern in m. 5 with that of the same pattern in m. 9.

---

*The kickbeat notation in which the dotted quarter note is preceded by a tied eight note

(_____) is similar to the notation of the syncopated quarter note pattern found in Duet 8

(_____). The two patterns differ in that, in the syncopated quarter note pattern, the dotted quarter is the second of two consecutively syncopated notes, while, in the kickbeat pattern, this configuration of two consecutive syncopations is not found.

The kickbeat pattern in which the dotted quarter note is preceded by an eighth note (_____) is similar to the notation of the tied eighth note anticipation found in Duet 5 in which the anticipatory eighth note is written as a dotted quarter note (_____ notated _____), especially in those instances in which the dotted quarter note is followed by note values rather than rest values. The tied eighth note anticipations can be distinguished from the kickbeat in music that contains articulative markings as the dotted quarter note would be shown accented. In those instances in which the articulation is not marked, the determination of the category of the pattern, and hence the accentuation, if any, is left to the discretion of the player and the manner in which he views the dotted quarter note within the context of the phrase. In ensembles, the phrasing of the lead player should be followed.

KICKIN' IT AROUND

DUET 25

Charleston Patterns

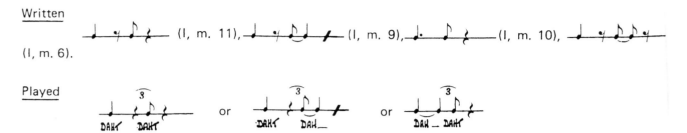

Written

(I, m. 11), (I, m. 9), (I, m. 10),

(I, m. 6).

Played

DAHT DAHT or DAHT DAH or DAH DAHT

Preliminary Exercises

1. Variations of the Charleston Pattern, beginning on the first beat of the measure. Compare m. 1 with m. 2, m. 5 with m. 6, and m. 9 with m. 10.

2. Charleston patterns beginning on the third beat of the measure.

Review

(I, m. 6) from Duet 13; (I, m. 26) from Duet 23; (I, m. 22) from Duet 24.

CHARLIE JACK

DUET 26

Charleston Patterns

Written

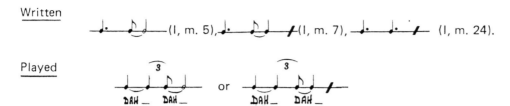

Played

Preliminary Exercise

With the pattern beginning on the first beat of the measure in m. 2 and 3, and the third beat of the measure in m. 6 and 7. Compare m. 1 with m. 2 and m. 5 with m. 6.

Review

──── (I, m. 18) from Duet 24. Compare m. 1 with m. 30.

SEPTEMBER'S SONG

DUET 27

Punctuation

Written*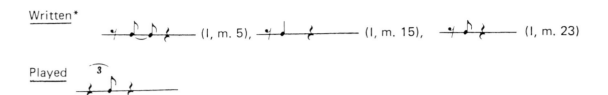

Played

Preliminary Exercise

    Compare m. 1 with m. 2, m. 2 with m. 3, m. 5 with m. 6, and m. 6 with m. 7. Mentally emphasizing the rest preceding the punctuation will help to accurately place these notes. Arrows point to these rests in the exercise below.

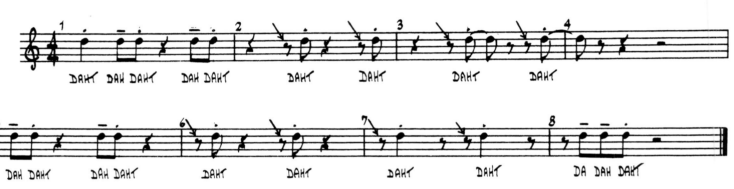

Review

     (I, m. 10), not a Charleston or kickbeat pattern, but a syncopated quarter note pattern from Duet 19; (I, m. 1), a Charleston pattern from Duet 26; (I, m. 20), a Charleston pattern from Duet 25.

    *The notation of the punctuation pattern is similar to that of the syncopated quarter note pattern found in Duet 13 in which an eighth rest is substituted for both eighth notes in the basic pattern ( ). In the syncopated quarter note pattern, the quarter note is followed by an eighth rest which is then followed by a note value ( ). In the punctuation pattern, the quarter note is followed by a quarter or larger rest value ( ).

SIPPIMISSI MUD

DUET 28

Individual Eighth Note Anticipations

Written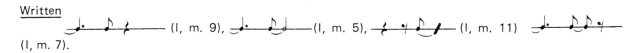

(I, m. 7).

Played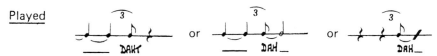

Preliminary Exercise

Compare m. 1 with m. 2, and m. 2 with m. 3. Accurace placement of the syncopated note will be aided by mentally emphasizing the downbeat preceding the anticipation. In the first line of the exercise below, an arrow points to this downbeat. Note that, to find the downbeat eighth note, the dotted quarter note should be regarded as a quarter note tied to an eighth note, as is shown above the staff.

Review

 (I, m. 20), punctuation from Duet 27.

MELODY FOR MICHELE

DUET 29

Quarter Note Triplets

Written 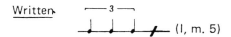 (I, m. 5)

Played

Quarter note triplets are given the same duration as in traditional music; that is, each note is held for two-thirds of a beat.

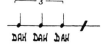

Preliminary Exercise

Compare m. 1, 2, and 3, one to another. Note the breakdown of the uneven beat division in line 2.

Review _____ (I, m. 14-15), from Duet 27; _____ (I, m. 31) from Duet 28.

LULL-A-BYIN' RHYTHM

DUET 30

Eighth Note Triplet Patterns
with Ties and/or Rests

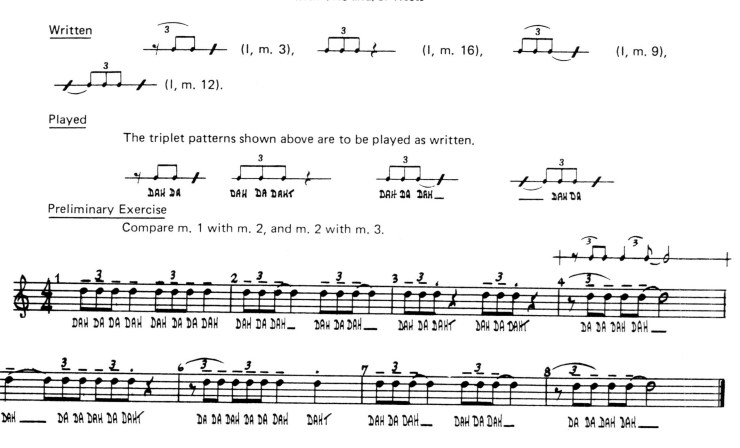

Written

Played

The triplet patterns shown above are to be played as written.

Preliminary Exercise

Compare m. 1 with m. 2, and m. 2 with m. 3.

Review

(I, m. 4), Charleston pattern from Duet 25; (I, m. 6), a syncopated quarter note pattern from Duet 12.

TRIPLICATION

MODERATELY SLOW BLUES